SHORT DESCRIPTION
OF
GODS, GODDESSES
AND RITUAL OBJECTS
OF
BUDDHISM AND HINDUISM
IN NEPAL

Compiled by
Jnan Bahadur Sakya

Handicraft Association of Nepal
P. O. Box 784, Kathmandu
Nepal

Published by : **Handicraft Association of Nepal**
P. O. Box 784
Kathmandu, Nepal
Tel. : 244231, 245467
Fax : 00977-1-222940
E-mail : han@wlink.com.np

ISBN 99933-373-3-1

1st Published On :-	1989	5000	Copies
2nd Edition :-	1991	8000	Copies
3rd Edition :-	1994	3000	Copies
4th Edition (Revised) :-	1995	5000	Copies
5th Edition (Reprint) :-	1996	10000	Copies
6th Edition (Reprint) :-	1998	10000	Copies
7th Edition (Reprint) :-	1998	10000	Copies
8th Edition (Reprint) :-	1999	10000	Copies
9th Edition (Reprint) :-	2000	20000	Copies
This Edition (Reprint) :-	2002	20000	Copies

Price:- Rs.80.00 Net

Printed at : **SUBHASH PRINTING PRESS**
Nakabahil, Lalitpur, Nepal
Phone : 533191

FORE WORD

Every handicraft businessman felt due need of a book which contains the descriptions of Gods, Goddesses and Ritual objects of Buddhism and Hinduism of Nepal. Hence the Handicraft Association of Nepal has decided to publish this sort of book which will enable to help and assist the business communities. Similarly, it enhances the promotion and development of dying away handicraft and metal craft industries.

We are grateful to UNDP and ESC whose moral and continuous support made this programme a grand success.

We are thankful to Mr. Jnan Bahadur Sakya of Nagbahal, Patan for his help in preparing this book in an efficient way.

We would be very happy to receive your valuable suggestions on its development.

We remain,

Handicraft Association of Nepal
P. O. Box 784
Kathmandu, Nepal
Tel. : 244231, 245467

PREFACE

The Handicrafts Association of Nepal has decided to publish a book with short description of Buddhist and Hindu Gods, Goddesses and ritual objects. The association gave me the opportunity to undertake this task. With the help of different scholars, publications and advice I could prepare this small book.

As I am not a scholar in this subject, there may be some mistakes. If any body finds the mistake I would be much grateful for the notice to me so to make correction in future. Though small, I hope that it will be helpful to some extend and, if, one finds it helpful I feel it a great success.

Lastly, I express my deep gratefulness to Mr. Tara Bahadur Sakya, President of the Handicrafts Association of Nepal for the opportunity given to me to undertake this task.

JNAN B. SAKYA

CONTENTS

Introduction of Buddhism and Hinduism

For two and a half thousand years, people have followed a religion based on the teachings of a man they called the Buddha, meaning the Enlightened One.

The starting point in Buddhism is mankind and the way in which they suffer not just physical pain but the general feelings of dissatisfaction with life, the craving to achieve or have something more, the fear of change and death. It seeks to give a person peace of mind and to encourage and develop loving compassion towards all living beings.

Buddhism is not a dogmatic religion in the sense that it does not require a person to accept fixed beliefs and ideas. It does not concern itself by debating whether or not there is a God. It regards all such beliefs as secondary importance. The main thing is to help people overcome suffering and to achieve a full life.

The goal of Buddhist religion is enlightenment which means to be fully awake to the reality of life, to have an understanding of why there is suffering in the world and how it may be overcome. Buddhists claim that in the teaching of the Buddha they find a path which will eventually lead them to achieve this enlightenment for themselves.

There is a great variety within Buddhism. There are two main Branches of the religion - Theravada or Hinayana Buddhism in the South and Mahayana Buddhism in the North. Nevertheless there is a common basis to all Buddhism expressed in what is called the Triple Jewel (Tri Ratna). The Buddha (the enlightened one), the Dharma (teaching) and the Sangha (community of monks.)

HINAYANA BUDDHISM

Difference of opinions and arguments arising from time to time caused the formation of new sects. Finally there arose two sects of thought which are known as Hinayana and Mahayana.

The Hinayana adhered more to the concept of four noble truths and eightfold paths which were primarily a philoshophy with rules of conducts and ethics. For them the worship of deities was secondary. The conception of Nirvana was the freedom from the cycle of rebirth.

Hinayana got it's name because this doctrine is meant for the individual salvation where each person has to work out his own destiny. comparatively few are able by their own efforts to obtain emancipation and achieve Nirvana. Hinayana Buddhism is also called Theravada Buddhism.

MAHAYANA BUDDHISM

Early Buddhism stressed that the goal of each individual was to seek freedom from the chain of rebirth and thus from all sufferings and death. The word used to describe this goal was Nirvana. Although there were many different philosophical schools, the religion centered around the institution of the monastery, with its ordained monks and a lay congregation that supported the monastery. The ritual were simple and minimum. Meditation and introspection were encouraged. Each individual sought his own Nirvana. Where as in Mahayana Buddhism the concept of Boddhisatwa, the being who desired highest enlightenment for the welfare of other and his practice of six Parmita (Dana, Sila, Kshanti, Birya, Dhyana, Prajna) is emphasised. The function of the Boddhisatwa was to postpone his own final leap into Nirvana and to remain in the round as long as a single sentient beings remained undelivered from suffering. This form of Buddhism came to be known as Mahayana (the great way) or the Boddhisatwayana.

The goal of Mahayana is to attain buddhahood. the method of attaining was modified. Buddhism changed through Mahayana into an altruistic faith oriented system in which in addition to meditative practices, devotion to a Boddhisatwa was regarded as an equally valid way to reach Buddhahood. The goal was now characterised as the state of Tatatha, emptiness and nonduality.

VAJRAYANA BUDDHISM

Mahayan which is dominated by Mantras is known as Mantrayana, Tantrayana or Vajrayana. It is characterised as the path which leads to perfect enlightenment. Vajrayana literally means the adamantine path or vehicle, but its technical meaning is the 'Sunya Vahicle' where Sunya is used to a special sense to represent vajra. Vajra also means 'Thunderbolt' or 'diamond' and Yana means 'Path, Way or Vehicle'.

Bajra, connoting diamond, was chosen as the name of the tantric Buddhist tradition because of the diamond's indestructability as well as of its physical ability to cut through all substances. Vajrayana constitutes the last major stage in the development of Buddhism.

Vajrayana Buddhism accepts all assumptions of Mahayana, but expands and elaborates them further adding a few of its own. The goal is now characterised as Boddhi Nature (the matrix of Enlightenment). Every sentient being is a potential Buddha, but he or she is unaware of it bacause of the dense fog of ignorance that clouds the mind. The fog is said to be discursive thought, which discriminates and polarises all concepts. Once it is moved Boddhi nature will emerge like a clear light. This state of reality it achieved by combining "Prajna" (Knowledge, wisdom or insight) with "Upaya" (means of fitness of action which is the same as karuna or compassion). Thus, both literally and figuratively, Vajrayana is the belief in the twin principles of insight and compassion and in their "Sahaja" (co-emergence) which leads one to the state of Mahasukha (greatbliss).

HINDUISM

Hinduism is a multi disciplinary religion called Sanatana Dharma based on writings and experiences of age old sages. They assert the view that a permanent, partless, independent self does exits.

There are endless divisions of Hindu systems; briefly, however, they are widely known to consist of six fundamental schools, Vaisesika, Naiyayika, Samkhya, Mimamsaka, Nirgrantha, and Lokayat (Carvaka). The first five of these hold views of eternalism (Sasvatavada) and the last holds view of nihilism (Echchedavada).

Hinduism also advocates different ethical systems and meditation systems. By praciticing these systems one can take rebirth in Brahma realm.

Ritual Objects

AGNI (Flame)

It is used as weapon of war and as an important component of offerings. It is often carried by Shiva. It may be held by the fire god Agni or may issue from his body.

ANKUSH (Goda)

It is made of small wooden handle topped by a strong and sharp metal hook. The handle is sometimes in the form of Vajra. It is the attribute of many tantric deities. When the goad is surmounted by a Vajra, it is called Vajrankush.

AKSHAMALA (Rosary)

It is a symbol of the never ending cycle. It is a string of beads. The beads are of a kind of seed of dried fruit. It may be made of other material also such as crystal. In Buddhist Tradition, it is a special symbol of Avalokiteswar. It is also a symbol of Prajnaparmita, Chunda, Vasundhara. In Hindu tradition, Brahma, Shiva, Ganesh and Saraswati also carry it.

BANA (Arrow)

Bana is an arrow. It is the symbol of awareness appears with tantric deities Marici, Kurukulla.

BINA (LUTE)

It is a stringed musical instrument. It is a favourite instrument of Saraswati, goddess of wisdom, learning and arts.

CHAITYA (Stupa)

Chaitya or the Stupa, which represents the Buddhist Universe, is the Buddhist sanctuary, sometimes square and sometimes round, with spires or steps on the capital. Each spire or step represents a heaven, the uppermost portion being a point which is supposed to be the highest peak of Mount Sumeru, a mythical mountain whence the Boddhichitta loses itself in sunya. On the four sides of the chaitya the figures of four Dhyani Buddhas Akshobhya, Ratna sambhav, Amitabha, Amoghasiddhi are placed. The place of Vairochana is in the centre. In some Chaitya Vairochana is placed to the east along with Akshobhya.

CHAKRA (Wheel)

Wheel is a symbol of absolute completeness. In the vedic times the wheel was symbolical of occult powers and symbol of Hindu god Vishnu or Krishna. In Buddhism, it symbolizes the wheel of the law which turns twelve times or three revolutions for each of the four noble truths. It is represented with eight spokes indicating the eight fold path of salvation.

CHANDRA (Moon)

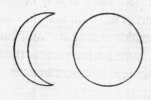

It appears often above the image of deities. In Buddhist Vajrayana tradition symbolizes complementary of opposites. Both Sambar and Shiva have the crescent moon as their hair dress.

KAPALA (Half Skull)

For containing blood in tantric ritual. Held by Kali and other manifestations of Shiva Sakti, by Mahakala and other guardian deities and their Dankinis. Kapala is made of severed head of a man or the cup made of a skull, or a bowl. The skull cup is of two kinds, when it is filled with blood it is called Asrkkapala, and when with flesh it is called Mamsa kapala. It is used in Tantric ritual. The deities are appeared to partake of the blood or the flesh of the demon carried in these cups.

VAJRA (Thunder Bolt)

The thunderbolt or diamond that destroys all kinds of ignorance, and itself is indestructible. The Vajra is symbol of Indra also. In tantric rituals, the Vajra symbolised the male principle which represents method in the right hand and the Bell symbolised the female principle, is held in the left. Their interaction leads to enlightement. Also the Dorje or Vajra represents the "Upaya" or method Tibetans name Vajra as "Dorje".

PA (Battle Axe)

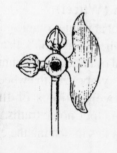

In Tantric Buddhist iconography, the battle axe is held by ferocious deities to symbolize severence of this worldly attachments. In Hindu Iconography, it is a weapon held in the hand of Parasuram, the sixth Avatar of Vishu, who descended to this world to fight Kshatriyas caste of warriors at the call of Bramins.

BELL

The bell representing the female aspect, stands for "prajna" or "wisdom". This is held in the left hand Dorje held in the right and they are always used in combination during the religious ceremonies. So Bell & Dorje are inseperable ritual objects and two together lead to enlightenment.

CHHATRA (Parasol)

It is a symbol of Buddhist goddesses such as Pancharaksa, Usnisasita. It protects from the evils. It is one of the eight symbols of good luck.

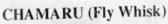

CHAMARU (Fly Whisk)

It is often held by supporting Hindu deities and semi devine beings and attendants. It is one of the eight symbols of good luck.

DIPA (Lamp)

It is sacred lamp fed with Ghee (butter). People offer it to the Gods and Goddesses.

DHOOP DANI
(Incense Burner)

It is a pot made of metal for burning incense which is to be offered to the gods and goddesses.

DAMARU (Drum)

It is a small double drum with a leather string tied over the narrow middle part of it, where knotted, wooden or bone ends make of rattling sound on the drum's memberances, when swung. It is appeared along with the trident (Trisula) in association with shiva cults. The tantric symbol known as the Damaru is a hand drum made of two half skulls.

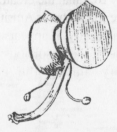

DHANUSA (Bow)

Dhanusa is a bow. It is generally carried in the left hand. It apprears with the tantric deities such as Marici, Kurukulla. With the bow and the arrow Marici inflicts pain to the Maras and wicked beings. Like Bajra and Ghanta, bow and arrow symbolize the complementary of method and wisdom.

DHWOJA (Banner)

It signifies the victory of Buddhism.

GADA (Mace)

A staff with a tapering end used as a weapon in close combat. It is a symbol of Vishnu. A club made of human bone with a skull on the end of it is carried by Devi, Durga, Kali and Bhairab.

KANGLING

A trumpet is made of human thigh-bone. It is a ritual object used at the time of tantric ceremony and blown to drive away evil spirits. Damaru goes side by side which gives "Magical Music" for the celestial journey. Music is considered to be similar to a mantra.

KALASA

In Hindu tradition, Kalasa contains the primeval water carried by Brahma, the creator. In Buddhist iconography, the Kalasa helds Amrit, the water or the elixir of immortality. It appears with Padmapani. It is also one of the auspicious sign and symbolizes plenty among the eight Astamangalas.

KARTIKA

A weapon symbolizing severance of all material and this worldly bonds held by Mahakala and by the Dankinis embracing the Dharmapalas and the Yidams such as Yama and Yamantaka.

KHADGA (Sword)

It is a symbol of enlightenment, used to destroy ignorance, the enemy of liberation from the bonds of worldly attachments, hence of contineous misery. It is a special symbol of Manjushree. The sword in the hand of Manjushree is called the Prajna Khadga or the sword of wisdom which is believed to destroy the darkness of ignorance by the luminous rays issuing out of it.

KHARTWANGA

It is a kind of club, made of bone of forearm or leg, sometimes of wood and metal. It is a magic wand held by tantric deities, Dakinis and Vajrayana saints. It is generally surmounted either by Vajra or Kapala or the Trishula or the banner or all of them. In any case for a Khatwanga the skulls are necessary and it will be so called even if nothing else in present.

LINGAM (Linga)

It is a symbol of Shiva. In its usual form it is a cylindrical piece of stone or wood standing on its narrow end. The top is usually rounded. The lingam is frequently founded in combination with the Yoni, a platelike disc with a drain, which supports the lingam.

(17)

MANDALA

Mandala (Literally meaning a circle) is a Tantric meditation device. It is a visual aid for concentration and introvertive meditation leading to the attainment of insights and to activation of forces culminating in "Siddhi" supernatural forces. The Mandala is the graphic representation of this process. It is not only theoritical but practical as an operational scheme involving a clear plan for practical realization of the process within oneself. It thus becomes an instrument (Yantra). There are many types and varieties of mandalas depending on the nature of the central deity. The most classic pattern of mandalas are of the Dhyani Buddha. This pattern appears in the oldest tantrics, The mandala repesents "Palace of Purity" a magic sphere cleansed of spiritual obstacles and impurities. The square of the 'sacred palace' proper is enclosed in multiple circles of flame, vajra, eight cemetries (appears only in wrathful deities) lotus, then the inner square to reach of the deity of the Mandala.

MATSYA (Fish)

It is a first incarnation of Vishnu, therefore may be associated with him. Suvarna matsya, the two golden fish, symbolizing beings rescued from the ocean of misery of earthly existence. It is also one of the eight auspicious signs of Astamangalas.

MAYURAPICCHA (Feathers)

It is a three peacock feathers spread in a kind of fan. The feathers are from the peacocks.

NAGA (Serpent)

Ramnant of early fertility rites. Worshipped as divine and semi-devine beings. Frequent ornament of guardian tantric deities. Nagas have power to bring or with held rain. So, they are regarded as gods of rain. They are believed to be the protector of the law of Buddha.

NAKULA (Mongoose)

A Mongoose vomiting jewels, is associated with god of wealth Kubera and his Buddhist counterpart, Jambala. It is believed to be the receptacle of all gems and when the god of wealth presses the animal, it vomits forth all the riches.

PADMA (Lotus)

Padma is a lotus which may be of any colour except blue. The blue lotus is designated by the word Utpala or Nilotpala. In Tantric works the Padma is the day lotus, while Utpala stands for the night lotus. It is regarded as especially sacred by all classes of Indians. When the lotus shows petals in both the upper and lower directions it is called the Viswapadma or the double lotus. Padma indicates purity of descent. In Buddhist tradition it symbolises self creation (Hence it is the sign of Swayambhu). In Vajrayana it represents the female principle. White open padma appears above the left shoulder of Avalokiteswara Padmapani, his spiritual Parents are Dhyani Buddha Amitabha and White Tara.

PHURPA

A "magic dart" used especially for the ritual slaying of human effigy of foe.

PRAYAR WHEEL

It is exclusively Buddhist praying instrument which always bears the mystical word "OM MANI PADME HUM' numbering six syllables in the mantra of Avalokiteswara. The syllables are carved outside the wheel as well as kept inside the wheel printed in the paper in numerous number. When it turns one round it means the mantra is read how much mantra has kept inside the wheel.

PUSTAKA (Book)

It is a symbol of transcendental wisdom accompanies both Buddhist and Hindu deities such as Brahma, Manjushree, Saraswati, Prajnaparamitta, Avalokiteswar, Vasundhara associated with wisdom, learning and arts. The book is sometimes placed on lotus. In Buddhist iconography, the Pustaka as a symbol represents the Prajnaparmita, a treaties on transcendent wisdom supposed to have been given to the Nagas by the Buddha to guard until mankind had become wise enough to grasp its profound truths.

SANKHA (Conch Sheel)

An offering vessel; a symbol of Vishnu. In Hindu tradition, the conch shell seems to have been extensively used in wars by ancient Indian. The white conch shell whose humming sound proclaims the glory of the saints. It is especially given as a symbol to the gods as the sounnd vibrated through a shell penetrates far and wide.

SHIELD

It represents Dharma which protects like a shield.

SHIRIVASTA

It is a endless knot. It is also considered luck knot, life knot or love knot.

SURYA (Sun)

It is a Hindu sun god. In Buddhism it is associated with moon as symbol of basic unity of the apparently different relative and absolute truth; appears separately in the upper part of thang-kas. It is a special symbol of Akashgarbha.

SWASTIKA

Used both in Hindusim and Buddhism as a symbol of the Law. It is also an auspicious sign (Swasti in Sanskrit is well being). It is one of the sixty five marks of Buddhahood found in the imprint of Buddha's foot. As a Buddhist symbol in represents the esoteric doctrine of Buddha.

VISWA VAJRA

When two thunderbolts are crossed it is called a Viswa Vajra. It is the emblem of Amoghasiddhi. In Buddhist Tantra the word generally disignates Sunya or Void which cannot be cut, cannot be destroyed but which destroys all evils.

TRI RATNA

It symbolizes the three fold Jewels namely Buddha, Dharma and Sangha. The meaning of these three fold jewels Buddha, Dharma and Sangha is a title signifying "The Enlightened" or "The Awakened", Buddha, the doctrine and community propounded by Shiddartha Gautam.

TRISULA (Trident)

It is also called Sula. It is the favourite weapon and the symbol of Shiva. The three forked weapon symbolizes Shiva's creation, protection, and destruction. It is carried by members of Shaivists. In Buddhist iconography, it is regarded as a representation of Tri Ratna, the three fold jewels - Buddha, Dharma and Sangha. It is also carried by Agni, Mahakala and Padma Sambhav.

UTPALA (Half Closed Lotus)

Elongated petals, blue, characterizes the Green Tara, consort of one of the Dhyani Buddha. It is designated by the word Utpala or Nilotpala. In tantric works Utpala stands for Night lotus. It is the special symbol of Manjushree and green Tara.

TANTRA

It is the name of the text which expound the mystic philosophy and the priniciples of action leading to the attainment of "Englightment" i.e. the state of mind of total independence from the bonds of existence in the span of one's life.

YAB-YUM

Yab-yum, is a Tibetan word consisting of two particles yab and yum. The word 'Yab' in Tibetan means the 'honourable father' and 'Yum' means the 'honourabhe mother'. The combined word therefore, means the father in the company of the mother or in her embrace.

YANTRA

(Shree Yantra)

Yantra is a nucleaus of the visible and knowable, a linked diagram of lines by means of which visualized energies are concentrated. There are different kinds of Yantras and Sri Yantra is the Great Yantra. Other lesser yantras (Om yantra, Kali yantras etc.) are obviously segments out of the all embracing Sri yantra. Yantras may be made in permanent form of many substances. The Most important is rock crystal. Its clear colourless substance which can be shaped so as to focus light at its apex in a very good emblem for the all, inclusive substance of fundamental reality just as colourless light includes all the possible colours of light. So crystal can serve as analogy for the substance which includes all substance.

MUKHA (Ritual Crown)

The crown worn by Buddhist priests of Vajrayana during the religious performances is known as Mukha (ritual crown). Invariably, the crown bears images of four of the five Dhyani Buddha to establish cosmic principle. The Dhyani Buddhas represented here are Vairochana, Akshyovya, Ratna Sambhaba, and Amitabha. The fifth member Amoghashiddhi is not shown physically but is symbolized by the thunderbolt at the top of the crown.

POORNA KALASH
(Full Vessel)

Poorna Kalash is a water vase which is full of all the characteristics of goodness As it is full of all goodness it is treated as an auspicious object for all human beings. When the religious ceremonies are held Poorna Kalash is kept at the centre surrounded by eight vessel. In Poorna Kalash, there will be the signs of eight auspicious symbols.

SUKUNDA (Oil lamp)

Sukunda is an oil lamp with combination of lamp and oil container. It is made of metal in artistic design. Oil was stored in the main section of the large pot and burnt in the bowl beside the neck with the aid of a wick. The filling of oil was done by a metal spoon known as Sumicha. Sukunda is the most important object for every religious and social performances. There must be the inscription of Ganesh in it, whose presense is always needed for the performances as the god of bestower of success.

GHAU (Prayer Box)

Ghau is a portable shrine in which an image of the owner's personal deity (Ishta Devata) is kept wrapped in silk cloth. Most Tibetans used Ghau at home and during travelling. At home, it is kept on an alter. But when travelling it is fastened at the cross belt. Generally, Ghau has a trefoil shapes top and a window in the middle through which one can see the personal deity. Ghau is made of two parts which fit together to form a box. The back is usually left plain and the front is richly decorated.

BHUMBA

Water is perhaps the most important both in Hindu and Buddhist ritual and is always present on the alter in a costly pot or in some other container. The pot whose shape is just like a flat shape jar with a pipe to bring out the water from the pot and which is richly decorated with precious stones and metals is known as Bhumba.

PADMASANA

Asana also means a throne or a pedestal. If the pedestal of lotus is arranged in single petal row it is called Padmasana. If the lotus petals are arranged in a double row it is called Viswapadmasana.

SINGHASANA

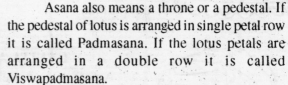

The pedestal supported by lion is called Sinhasana.

KURMASANA

The pedestal supported by the tortoise is called Kurmasana.

SAYANA ASANA

It is a sleeping pose of Hindu god Vishnu.

NRITYAMURTI ASANA

A pose of dancing Shiva and other various tantric gods are found in this position.

ASANA (Sitting Position)

DHYANA ASANA

The Meditative pose is also called padmasana. In this position the legs are crossed closely locked with the soles of both feet visible. All Buddhas and Bodhisatwas seated are found in this position.

LALITA ASANA

A pose of ease-one leg pendant and often resting on a lotus flower. The other leg is in the usual position of Buddha. Taras, the consort of Dhyani Buddha, Saraswati, Basundhara are found in this Asana.

PARYANKA ASANA

The Europeon position seated knees apart and both legs pendent. The position of Maitriya Buddha.

RAJALILA ASANA

Seated with right knee raised and left leg in the usual position of Buddha. Right arm hanging loosly over the right knee. Hindu deities are often shown in this posture.

ASANA (Standing Postures)

SAMAPADA ASANA

A pose standing either in straight or in various degrees of flexion of body or legs. Boddisatwas are found in this position.

ALIDH ASANA

A pose stepping to the left with right leg straight and left leg bent. The aggressive forms of god, the Dakinis and the wrathful deities are found in this position.

MUDRA (Gesture)

ABHAYA

Abhaya Mudra is the Mudra (Gesture) of Protection. In this gesture, the arm is elevated and slightly bent. The hand is lifted to shoulder level with the palm turned outward and all the fingers are extended upward. This mudra is characteristic of Dhyani Buddha Amoghsiddhi.

BHUMISPARSA

Bhumisparsa is the mudra of witness (earth-touching). The right arm is pendant over the right knee. The hand with the palm turned inward and all the fingers extended downward with the finger touching the lotus throne. The left hand lies on the lap with palm upward. This gesture 'of touching the earth' or calling the earth to witness' commemorating Gautam Buddha's victory over temptation by the demon Mara.

This gesture is Characteristic of Dhyani Buddha Akshobhya as well as Shakyamuni.

DHARMACHAKRA

Dharmachakra Mudra is the gesture of Teaching. Literally, Dharma means 'Law' and Chakra means wheel and usually interpreted turning the Wheel of Law. In this gesture both hands are held against the chest, the left facing inward, covering the right facing outward, the index and thumb of each hand making a circle. It is characteristic of Dhyani Byddha Vairochana. It is also a gesture of hands exhibited by Lord Buddha while preaching his first sermon at Sarnath.

DHYANA MUDRA

Dhyana Mudra is the Mudra of Meditation. It is also called Samadhi or Yoga Mudra. Both hands are placed on the lap, right hand on left with fingers fully stretched and the palms facing upwards. Often, a begging bowl is placed. This is the characteristic mudra of Dhyani Buddha Amitabha.

JNANA MUDRA

Jnana Mudra is the gesture of teaching. In this gesture, the tips of the index and the thumb are joined and held near the center of chest with the palm turned inward. This is the characteristic mudra of Manjushree.

NAMASKAR MUDRA

Namaskar Mudra is the gesture of prayer. In this gesture, the hands are kept closed to the chest in devotional attitude with the palms and fingers joined. This is the special gesture of Avalokiteswara when with more than two arms.

TARJANI MUDRA

Tarjani Mudra is the gesture of threatening or warning. Only the index finger is raised while the other fingers are locked up in the fish. This mudra is characteristics of most of the wrathful deities.

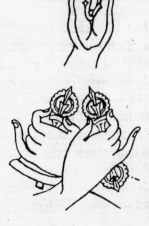

VAJRAHUNKARA MUDRA

Vajrahunkara Mudra is the gesture of Adi Buddha, Vajradhara. In this gesture the wrists are crossed at the breast. The hands hold usually the Vajra and Ghanta. This is the special mudra of Vajradhara and Samvara and most of the gods when holding their Saktis.

VARADA

Varada Mudra is the gesture of Charity or conferring boon or grace. The arm is extended all way down with palm facing outwards, fingers extended downwards. This is the Mudra of Dhyani Buddha Ratna Sambhava, Avalokiteswara, sometimes, of a standing Sakyamuni.

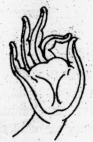

VITARKA MUDRA

Vitarka Mudra is the gesture of argument. In this gesture the tips of thumb and index finger touched forming a circle. All the other fingers are extended upwards. This is the mystic gesture of Taras and Boddhisatwas.

Gods and Goddesses
of Buddhism and hinduism

ADIBUDDHA

Adibuddha is the original Buddha who is without beginning and without end. He is said to be infinite, self created and revealing himself in the form of a blue flame coming out of a lotus. In Nepal, Swayambhu is worshipped as Adibuddha.

AMITABHA

Amitabha is the most ancient Buddhas among the Dhyani Buddhas. He said to reside in the Sukhabati heaven in peaceful medition. He is of red colour originating from the red syllable HRIH. He represents cosmic element of Sanjna (name). His vehicle is peacock. He exhibits Samadhi Mudra with his two palms folded face up one on top of the other lying on his lap. He has a lotus as his sign. When represented on the stupa, he always faces the west. He is worshipped thinking that one can have salvation. Sometimes holding a Patra on the same posture. His female is Pandara. Amitabha denotes "Boundless light" or Incomprehensible.

(30)

AMOGHSHIDDHI

Amoghshiddhi is the fifth Dhyani Buddha in order. His left hand lies open on the lap and the right exhibits the Abhaya mudra. He represents cosmic element of Samskar (Conformation). He is of green colour and his recognition symbol is the viswa vajra or the double thunderbolt. He always faces the North. He is the embodiment of the rainy season. Sometimes a serpent with seven heads forms the background as an umbrella. In front of his shrines, therefore, is found a small square pit which is meant for the snake. His vehicle is garud.

AMOGHAPASA LOKESWAR

Amoghpasa Lokeswar is also a form of Avalokiteswar. He is four-faced and eight - armed and stands on a lotus. He carries in his four right hands the Vajra, the sword, the goad and the bow, while the four left carry the Ghanta, the Trindandi, the noose and an arrow.

AKSHOBHYA

Akshobhya is next importance among the Dhyani Buddhas. He is regarded as the second Dhyani Buddha by the Nepalese Buddhists. Akshobhya originates from the blue syllable Hum. He is two-armed and one-faced and exhibits the Bhusparsa (earth touching) mudra which means calling the earth for witness, and sits in the Vajraparyanka pose. He represents the primordal cosmic element of Vijnana (consciousness). When represented in the Stupa, he always faces the east. His left hand rests on the lap, while the right rest on the right knee with the tip of the middle fingers touching the ground with palm drawn inwardly.

His vehicle is a pair of elephant and his recognition symbol is the vajra or the thunderbolt. His female is Locana.

ARDHANARISWARA

Ardhanariswara is combined form of god and goddess. When the image of half Shiva and half Gauri, it is called Hara Gauri. Like that half Vishnu and half Laxmi is popularly known as Laxmi Narayan.

AVALOKITESWARA

Among the 108 forms of Lokeswara Avalokiteswara is one who refuses to accept Nirvana since he considers such acceptance selfish in view of the ignorance of the great majority of the people who have not yet attained that stage. His sacrifice symbolises infinite compassion (Karuna), sharing of mankind's misery, willingness to help those in distress. He holds in his hand the indestructible jewel. He is saviour and protector from danger, So, his invocation (Mantra) "OM MANI PADME HUM" is found inscribed on rocks, loose stones, prayer wheels, etc. Avalokiteswara is called Chengresik in Tibet.

VAJRASATWA

Vajrasatwa, the sixth Dhyani Buddha, is regarded by the Nepali Buddhist as the priest of the Five Dhyani Buddha. He is not represented in the stupa like other Dhyani Buddhas, but independent shrines are dedicated to his worship. His worship is always performed in secret and is not open to those who are not initiated into the mysteries of the Vajrayana. Vajrasattwa is represented in two forms, single and yabyum. This

(32)

Dhyani Buddha wears all ornaments, rich dress and a crown. He is of white colour. He sits cross legged in the meditative pose like other Dhyani Buddhas. He carries the vajra in his right hand with palm upwards against the chest and ghanta (bell) in the left hand resting upon the left thigh.

BHAIRAB

Bhairab has a number of different forms. He is Shiva's another form in a terrible position and the most distinctive tantric form of Shiva. He is nude, black or dark blue in color. Sometimes in painting, he is white. He has rolling eyes, many arms but usually one head. In his hands are weapons, skull-cup, a wand with 3 skulls or a noose. He wears a necklace, garland of skulls and has skulls in his crown. His hair is unruly. He may wear sandals and is often standing on a recumbent figure.

BISWARUPA

A representation of many gods in one. He is a many-headed, many armed. The rear circle of arms has the hands in all the various hand-poses; other circles hold all the implements and weapons. All the heads terrible and gentle are those of the deities.

CHAKRA SAMBARA

Chakra Sambara is the main deity of Sambara. He is also regarded as manifestation of Heyvajra who is the central figure of an esoteric cult, the Vajrayana Buddhism. Vajrabarahi is his consort embracing in a mystic position. Their embrace symbolises union between wisdom and method which leads ultimate bliss.

CHANDAMAHAROSHANA

Chanda Maharoshan is also called Maha chandrarosana and Acala. He is one faced, two armed and squint eyed. His face appears terrible with bare fangs. He wears a jewelled head-dress, bites his lips and wears on his crown a garland of severed heads. His eyes are slightly red. He carries the sword in his right hand and the noose round the raised index finger against the chest in the left. His sacred thread consists of a white snakes. He is clad in tiger skin and he wears jewels. His left leg touches the ground, while the right is slightly raised. His worship is always performed in secret and the god is kept secluded from public gaze. He is emanated of Akshobhya, so he bears on his crown the effigy of Akshobhya.

CITIPATI (TWO SKELETONS)

The Citipati is two skeletons, one is a male and the other is a female. They are represented with arms and legs interlaced, dancing on two corpses. Each holds a wang topped by a skull. One holds a skull cup and the other a vase. Sometimes both carries the same symbol. According to the Buddhist legend, the citipati were two ascetics in their former existence. Once they were lost in a deep meditation, they did not notice that a thief had cut off their heads and thrown them in the dust. Since then they became ferocious enemies of the thief and had vowed eternal vengeance.

CHINTAMANI LOKESWAR

He is also a form of Lokeswar who dispenses jewels and wealth to his devotees. He is the Lokeswar of wishing gem.

DAKINI

A class of demon goddess, female versons of male dakas. Dakini literally means "sky walking woman', hence believe that can fly. Also it is used as synonym for prajna; therefore, as the embodiment of wisdom, every goddess are regarded as dakini. They are further used to designate the female partner in the tantric initiation, and thus she can be both human and superhuman.

DIKPALAS

Dikpalas are the guardians of four direction and four corners. Indra, king of gods, presides over the East; Varuna, lord of ocean, over the West; Kubera, God of wealth, over the North and Yama, God of death, over the South: The regents of the four corners are Agni, God of fire, who rules the Southeast; Vayu, God of wind, rules the Northwest; Isana, a form of Shiva, rules the Northeast and Nairitya, God of dread, rules the Southwest. No independant cult evolved around these eight divine gaurdians, but like the Navagrahas they are invoked in every religious ritual, especially those associated with buildings.

DHYANI
BUDDHAS
(Pancha Buddhas)

DHYANI Buddhas are emanated from Adibuddha. There are five Dhyani Buddhas (Buddhas in Meditation). They are not separate gods. They are just abstract aspects of Buddhahood. They are also often Called Tathagata. They are so popular in Nepal that they are found in every stupa, thousands of Chaityas (small stupas), in courtyards, and found painted in the main entrance of the Buddhist house. In Kathmandu, they are also called Panch Buddhas. They are always shown seated in the position of meditation. Of the five Dhyani Buddhas the senior is Vairochana who occupies centre of the Mandala. In the Chaityas only four other Dhyani Buddhas the senior is Vairochana who occupies centre of the Mandala. In the chaityas only four other Dhyani Buddhas Akshobhya in the east, Ratna Sambhav in the South, Amitabha in the west, and Amoghsidhi in the north are depicted.

DIPANKAR

Dipankar Buddha is a deity of Mahayana Buddhism. He is the 'Enlightener' and one of the earliest of the many assumed predecessors of Gautama Buddha added as the twenty fifth. He is said to have come from Deepavati, a mythological city. At the moment of his birth there was a miraculas manifestation of a large number of bright lamps (Dipa), hence he was named Dipankar.

Dipankar Buddha is believed to have lived 100000 years on earth. Dipankar Buddha represented with the right hand in Abhaya Mudra and left shows the Varada. He is either sitting or standing with the monastic garment drapped over the left shoulder with pleated edges, where as the lower garments is pleated in a manner of a flowering skirt.

DURGA

Durga is a wrathful form of Parvati. She is also known as Mahishamardini, one who killed the demon Mahisha. She is represented with many arms with a weapon in each hand. Her right foot is supported by her mount, the lion, the left poised on the subdued demon, her left hand holding the tail of her victim, thrusts the trident into the body of the demon killing him apparently at the very moment when he is about to draw his sword in self defence. She is sometimes shown setting astride on her mount, the lion with four hands holding a sword, a club, a lotus flower and a dire. Her face always remains calm and gentle.

EKADAS LOKESWAR

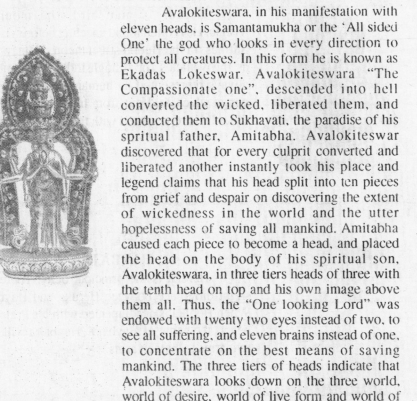

Avalokiteswara, in his manifestation with eleven heads, is Samantamukha or the 'All sided One' the god who looks in every direction to protect all creatures. In this form he is known as Ekadas Lokeswar. Avalokiteswara "The Compassionate one", descended into hell converted the wicked, liberated them, and conducted them to Sukhavati, the paradise of his spritual father, Amitabha. Avalokiteswar discovered that for every culprit converted and liberated another instantly took his place and legend claims that his head split into ten pieces from grief and despair on discovering the extent of wickedness in the world and the utter hopelessness of saving all mankind. Amitabha caused each piece to become a head, and placed the head on the body of his spiritual son, Avalokiteswara, in three tiers heads of three with the tenth head on top and his own image above them all. Thus, the "One looking Lord" was endowed with twenty two eyes instead of two, to see all suffering, and eleven brains instead of one, to concentrate on the best means of saving mankind. The three tiers of heads indicate that Avalokiteswara looks down on the three world, world of desire, world of live form and world of no form.

GANESH

Ganesh, the elephant headed god of wisdom and success is the defender and remover of obstacles and has to be propitiated first before worship to other gods. He is one of the sons of Shiva. He is known as "Sidhi Data" or bestower of success in the work. His elephant head has only one full tusk, while the other is broken. He said to have lost it in a fight with Parasuram. It is also said that he broke it to write the Mahabharata to the dictation of sage Vyasa. His elephant head is believed to be an emblem of wisdom and his mount an emblem of sagacity. His mount is the "Mooshika" called shrew. He is also known as Vinayaka.

GARUDA (BANTEJ)

Garuda is man bird, the mount of Vishnu. He is often found kneeling before Vishnu's Shrines. In the Buddhist Pantheon, he may serve as the Vehicles for Amoghsiddhi. He is almost always represented as human, except for large wings which fold out from his shoulders. Some times he is represented with the head of a bird.

HAYBAJRA

Heruka is the principal deity. There is a slight difference between Heruka and Haybajra. When Heruka is accompanied with his Prajna, he begets the name of Haybajra. Haybajra will have two arms to sixteen arms.

GREEN TARA

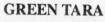

The Green Tara is regarded as spiritual consort of Amogasiddhi, the Dhyani Buddha. She is portrayed similar to that of the White Tara. One can find the difference only in her left hand which holds a half-closed lotus or water-lily flower with long petals which is often blue. In the Lamaeist Tradition, Tara is incarnated in all good women. She is also to have mortal base in historic persons of the Nepali and Chinese princess who married the great king Srang-Tsan Gampo and credited with the introduction of Buddhism to Tibet and China. She is worshipped, because she brings all good women. One of the main Tara in this group is Aryatara.

HARI HARIHARIVAHAN LOKESWAR

Harihariharivahan Lokeswar is also a form of Lokeswar, lowermost is the snake, above it is the lion, over the lion is a Garuda, Narayan rides Garuda, and on his shoulder is Lokeswar. The Garuda has two hands in the Anjali Mudra. Narayan has four hands, of which the first pairs engaged in forming the Anjali against the chest; while the second pair has the chakra in the right hand and the Gada in the left. Lokeswar sits in the vajra paryanka and has six arms with rosary, chakra, varada pose in the right and Tridandi, noose and utpala in the left.

HAYANGRIVA

Hayangriva is another deity emanated from Akshyobhya. He is of red colour, with eight arms and three faces, each face with three eyes. His right and left faces are blue and white respectively and he has snakes as ornaments. His first face has a swiling appearance, the right has a protuding tongue and he bits his lips in his left. He is cladded in tiger skin and shown in his four right hands the Vajra, the staff, the karana pose and the raised arrow. Of the four left hands, one has the raised index finger the second touches the breast and two remaining ones hold the lotus and the bow.

HERUKA

The number of deities emanating from the Dhyani Buddha Akshyobhya is quite large. All the emanations of Akshyobhya have a terrible appearance with distorted face, bare fangs, three blood shed eyes, protuding tongue, garlands of severe heads and skulls, tiger skin and ornaments of snake.

Among the deities emanating from the Dhyani Buddha Akshyobhya, Heruka stands

prominent. Heruka is worshipped singly as well as Yabyum. When he is in yab yum, he is generally known as Heyvajra. The worship of Heruka is said to confer Buddhahood on his worshippers. He is said to destroy all the Maras of the world.

INDRA

Indra is the Hindu God. He is the king of Heaven. He is regarded as a God of rain.

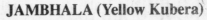

JAMBHALA (Yellow Kubera)

God of wealth, the Buddhist form of Kubera. As Yi-dam is called Jambala, probably from the Jambhara (Lemon) which he carries in his right hand. He is rather fat and prosperous looking. He holds a money bag and coins. His crown may contain an image of Ratnasambhava. Like Kubera, he is attended by a mongoose that vomits jewels. There is a white form of jambhala holding a trident and sceptre. He is seated sideways on a dragon.

KALACAKRA

Kalacakra in a Yi-dam (god potector) who turns the wheel of life. Kalacakra is the title of a work in one of the division of the Kangyur. It is possible that Kalacakra is a personification of that work. Kalacakra is usually as a Yidam with four head on each of which is a third eye. He may have twelve or twenty four arms but never has more than two legs. In his Yi-dam form he is dark blue. His body is covered by a tiger skin. He wears a belt formed of Vajras. He is always represented stepping to the left on two prostrate personges or demon, with four arms. The personage under the right foot holds a bow and arrow the one under the left a trident and Khatvanga.

KALI

She is a wrathful form of Parvati. She is the goddesss of mysteries. She is usually black or dark blue in colour. She is represented without dress except for garland of severed heads, tongue protrudes from her mouth. This goddess is worshipped in southern part of Nepal

BAJRAYOGINI

Bajrayogini is an important and popular Goddess. She has three forms in number and conform to two distinct types different from each other. In one form she has no head, but carries it in her hand and in another, she has her head intact. The former form is identical in appearance with the Hindu goddess Chhinamasta of the group of the Mahavidyas. She is always accompanied by the two yoginis on either side of her. She is yellow in colour. She carries in her left hand her own head severed by herself with her own katri held in her right hand. She is nude and her right leg is stretched, while the left is bent down. The another form is of red colour. She is no less terrible than the headless form. She is surrounded on all sides by the terrible burning grounds. She stands in the Alidha attitude, she rides the corpse. She is nude and has three red eyes and round contorted brows, protuding belly and tongue. She carries the kapala in the left hand and the Vajra in the right. The Khatwanga hangs from her left shoulder. This form of Vajrayogini is similar in many respects to the form of Nairatma and Vajravarahi.

KUBERA

The lord of wealth and gaurdian of the Northern Direction. According to the Hindu mythology, he is said to have performed austerities for a thousand years, in regard for which Bramha gave immortality and made him the god of wealth, gaurdian of all the treasures of the earth which he has to distribute according to the destiny of the receivers. Kubera's dwelling place was said to be on Alaka in the Himalayas, abounding in wealth and magnificent. Kubera is also worshipped by Buddhist

(41)

KUMARA

In Hindu mythology Kumara is known as Kartikeya. He is Ganesh's younger brother although neither of them is the natural son of Uma (consort of Shiva). Mounting his peacock and generally having six hands Kumara is the divine general god. In Hindu mythology, he is also represented as Skanda, the God of war.

LAXMI

Laxmi is goddess of wealth. She is usually found seated than standing. She has four hands among which the prominent two hands are in varada and Abhaya Mudra. The rest two hold Darpana (mirror) and Sinhamoo (Vermillion pot). She is always accompanied by two dwarfs. The new moon night of November is dedicated for her annual ceremony.

LHA MO (Chhwaskamuni)

Lha Mo is the only feminine divinity amongs the eight terrible ones. (Dharma Palas). She is an important goddess of the Tibetans. In many monasteries, she has a place on the corner. She is always kept behind the curtain. She is most terrifying manifestation in the Northern Buddhist Pantheon. Being the only goddess defender of the Mahayana school she was armed by the gods. Heybajra gave her two dice to determine the life of men. Brahma gave her a fan of peacock's feathers. Kubera gave her a lion, which she wears in her right ear. Nanda, the serpent god gave her a serpent, which hangs from her left ear. Vajrapani gave her a hammer. Other gods gave her a mule, whose covering is the skin of a demon and the reins are of venomous serpents. Lha Mo is represented seated sideways on her mule. She wears all the Dharmapala ornaments. She has the third eye. Her expression is ferocious. She wears a long garland of heads. Her covering is a tiger skin. In her right upraised hand, she displays the sceptre while the left holds the skull cup at the breast.

MAHASIDDHAS

Mahasiddhas are great successful Tantric Saints. They appear in numerous stories and texts which recount their lives. They are the one who had live successful Tantric lives performing innumerable rituals. One of the most important is Padma Sambhav, the founder guru of the Red Hat Sect in Tibet in the ninth century A. D. The word Maha signifies greatness and Siddha denotes a perfected being. Both Hindu and Buddhist tantras assert that by practicing certain rites, a person can gain control (Siddhi) over forces of Nature as well as acquire special abilities such as the ability to fly or to generate storm.

MAITREYA BUDDHA

Maitreya Budha is a future Buddha who is expected to come to earth from Tushita Heaven. He is supposed to be passing the life of a Bodhisatwa in the Tushita Heaven preparatory to his descent to earth in Human form. It is said that he will come to earth full 4000 years after the disappearance of Gautam Buddha for the deliverence of all sentient beings. He is the only Bodhisatwa who is worshipped both by the Hinayanists and the Mahayanists.

Maitreya may be represented as a standing figure adorned with rich ornaments and holding in his right hand the stalk of a lotus. Maitreya may also be represented seated as a Buddha, with legs either interlocked or dangling down. His colour is yellow, and his images sometimes bear the figures of Dhyani Buddhas.

MANJUSHREE

Majushree - "God of Divine Wisdom", whose worship confers mastery of the Dharma, retentive memory, mental perfection and eloquence. Manjushree is also one of the forms of Bodhisatwas and he symbolies wisdom. In Nepal, he is considered as the founder of Nepalese civilization and the creator of Kathmandu Valley. According to the tradition, he was a Chinese Saint. His intuition told him of the blue flame (symbolizing Adibuddha or Swayambhu) on a lotus in the big lake of Nepal. He went there to offer worship, but could not reach because of the water. He cut with his sword the southern wall of the hills. The water of the lake drained to the south. The dry valley became the Kathmandu Valley. He carries the sword of wisdom and light in his right hand and Prajnaparmita manuscipt "the book of Divine Wisdom" on his left on the lotus blossom. His left hand will be in teaching gesture (Jnan Mudra.) He is also called Manjunghose, Manju Bara, Vajranga and Vagiswara. People believe that the worship of Manjushree can confer upon them wisdom, memory, intelligence etc.

MAYADEVI

Mayadevi is the mother of Siddhartha Gautam and wife of king Suddhodana of Kapilavastu, west of Nepal.

LOKESWARA

Lord of the world form of Avalokiteswara, This form is assumed when Buddhist pantheon incorporated on Shiva. He is found both as an attendant deity and in his own shrine. He is richly ornamented. He wears a sacred thread of jewels and earrings. There will be full blown lotus at each shoulder.

MAHALAXMI

Mahalaxmi is one of eight mother goddesses, who mounts a lion and with many weapons identifies as a form of the great Goddess, Durga. Mahalaxmi holds in her sixteen arms (clockwise from the uppermost left hand) shield kettledrum, bow, waterpot, book, noose, gesture of admonition and exposition, skull cup, gesture of charity, lotus, trident, rosary, arrow, bell and sword. Mahalaxmi (Great Laxmi) is the presiding deity of one of the three sections of the Devi Mahamatya.

Although the goddess is equipped with various lethal weapons, she is not a menacing figure. Rather she appears quite placid and relaxed as she sits on her lion.

MEGH SAMBARA

Megh Sambara is a god of protection against enemies. He is portrayed with Buffalo head. He is also regarded as Buddhist Gaurdian god. He will be in conjunction with female principle or sakti, symbolising the union between wisdom and method. He is regarded as the wrathful form of Manjushree in the full expression of his powers.

MILA - RASPA

Milaraspa was a medicant monk and poet. He lived in the begining of the twelfth century. He spent his life wandering through Tibet performing miracles, converting the nomadic people to Buddhism and writing his 100000 songs. Milaraspa is represented in the bronzes seated on a gazelles skin on a lotus asana. He has short, curly hair, and is dressed in monastic garments. He always holds his right hand with the fingers extended and the palm turned outwards behind his right ear, as if he was listening to the echoes of nature. His left hand holds a begging bowl.

NAGA KANYA

The Nagas are the rain-givers, the guardians of the water. They also considered the guardians of the riches of the deep, and are supposed to carry a precious jewel in their foreheads. The daughter of Nagas are known as Naga Kanyas. The upper part of the body of Naga Kanya is of human, lower part is of a snake.

NAMASANGITI

Namasangiti is emanation of Vairochana. Like the goddess Prajnaparamita who is the embodiment of the Prajnaparmita literature, Namasangiti also seems to be the deification of the Namasangiti literature of the Buddhist pantheon. He is one faced, white in colour, has eyes (half closed) in meditation, a smiling contenance, the jata mukuta and various ornaments, is decked in the six auspicious ornaments, and twelve armed. He sits in the meditative pose on the lotus.

NARSIMHA

The man-lion is the forth incarnation of Vishnu. He is a killer of Hiranya Kasyapu, who was so strong that he could be slain by no-one except Narsimha.

PADMAPANI LOKESWARA

Padmapani Lokeswara is also a form of Bodhisatwa attached to the Padma (lotus) family which is presided over by the Dhyani Buddha Amitabha. Padmapani is of red colour and recognition symbol is full blown lotus.

PADMA SAMBHAV

Padma Sambhav was a renowned and highly learned tantric saint of Northern India. In the middle of the eight century the Tibetan King Thi-Sron Detsan sent to India inviting the learned guru to come to Tibet. Padma Sambhav was renowned for his knowledge of tantras and of their efficacious application. He remained 50 years in Tibet founding monasteries and teaching the tantra doctrine. He is said to have subdued all the malignant gods in the Tibet sparing only those that became converted to Buddhism and that promised to be defenders (Dharmapala) of the doctrine. Padmasambhav. in his turn, promised to enroll them in the Mahayana Pantheon. He claimed to have received from the dakini the books from which he acquired his miraculous power. At the end of fifty years Padma sambhav disappeared miraculously.

Padmasambhav is represented seated on a lotus asana with the legs locked, the right hand holding the vajra and the left, lying in his lap, the patra. He holds his special symbol, the khatvanga pressed against his breast with the left arm.

NAVAGRAHAS

Surya (Sun), Chandra (Moon), Mangal (mars), Buddha (Murcury) Brishaspati (Jupiter). Sukra (Venus), Sani (Satrun), Rahu and Ketu are Navagrahas or the Nine Planets. Rahu is a demon who cause eclipses of the Sun and the Moon. Ketu literally means 'Comet'. Since astrology plays an important role in the life of the Nepalese, the Navagrahas are frequently encountered in it. They appeared during every ceremony or rite whether religious or social.

PRAJNAPARMITA

Prajnaparmita is the Goddess of superior wisdom and transcendental intuition. She is regarded as the goddess who has thorough and complete knowledge of Bodhijnana or enlightened knowledge. She is the most popular one among the Vajrayana deities. She is usually shown in lotus posture. She has four arms with book on the upper left hand and rosary in the right hand while lower hands are in Dharma Chakra mudra.

RATNA SAMBHAV

Ratna Sambhav is regarded third Dhyani Buddha in order. His recongition symbol is the jewel and he exhibits the Varada Mudra (gift bestowing). He represents the cosmic element of vedana (sensation) and is the embodiment of slander. He is yellow in colour and always faces the south. His left hand rests on the lap with open palm and right exhibits the varada mudra or the gift bestowing attitude. His female counter part is Mamaki.

RAMAKRISHNA

Ramakrishna was a priest of the kali Temple of Dakshineswar. He devoted himself solely to the pursuit of spiritual knowledge to gain eternal peace. "The goal of human life is to see God" was his main teaching. So he practiced Tantric Sadhana, Advaita, Vedanta, Christianity and Islam to see the God, and in every practice he adept in no time. Men and women from all walks of life came to him. He trained a band of young men headed by Swami Vivekananda to carry his spiritual mission. He passed away at the age 50 in 1886.

SAMANTABHADRA

There are three groups with sixteen Bodhisatwas. Among these three groups one group is headed by Samanta Bhadra (Universal goodness). So he is important as the leader of sixteen Boddhisatwas. He is not less important than the Future Buddha Maitreya who is head of the two other lists of Boddhisatwas. He embraced by his consort "Dharmavajra"

SAKYAMUNI

Gautam Buddha is believed to have had 550 incarnations. Many previous Buddhas and other Buddhas yet to come are known as Buddhas. To distinguish from all other Buddhhas, he has been called Sakyamuni (The lion of Sakya clan), the son of king Suddhodana and queen Mayadevi. He was born on 563 B. C. at Lumbini, western part of Nepal. He had attained "Bodhi" or knowledge after 6 years in fasting and meditation and then he was called "Buddha" as he was "the enlightened one" He died at the age of 80 at Kusinagara.

VAJRADHARA

In Vajrayana, Adi Buddha is regarded as the highest deity of the The Buddhist Pantheon. When represented, he begets the name of Vajradhara and is conceived in two forms, single and yabyum. When single he is decorated with jewels, ornaments and dressess. He sits in the vajraparyanka or the attitude of meditation. He carries the vajra in the right hand and the ghanta in the left, the two hands being crossed against the chest as vajrahunkara mudra. In yabyum, his form remains the same as when single except that here he is locked in close embrace by his Sakti.

VAJRAVARAHI

Vajravarahi is a goddess whose colour is red. She has two arms. She exhibits in her right hand the vajra along with the raised index finger and shows in the left the Kapala and the Khatwanga. She is one faced and three eyed dishevelled hair is marked with the six auspisious symbols and is nude. She is the essence of the five kinds of knowledge, and is the embodiment of the Sahaj pleasure. She stands in the satyalidha attitude tremples upon the gods Bhairav and Kalratri, wears a garland of head still wet with blood which she drinks to quench her thirst.

VAIROCHANA

Vairochana is regarded as first Dhyani Buddha by the Nepalese Buddhist. His place is in the sanctum of the stupa where he is the master of whole temple and its contents. Therefore, he cannot be represented outside the stupa, but exception to this rule is frequently met within the important stupa of Nepal where he is assigned a place between Akshobhya in east and Ratna Sambhav in the south

Vairochana represents the cosmic element of Rupa (form). When represented, he is white in colour, and his two hands are held against the chest with the tips of the thumbs and forefingers of each hand united. His female is Vajradhatviswari. He is in preaching attitude.

TSON-KA-PA

Tson-ka-pa was born in Tibet in the middle of the fourteenth century and it is said that the tree which overshadowed the house in which he was born had the imprint of a Buddha on its leaves. Tson-ka-pa was a Northern Buddhist reformer. He founded the Gelugpa sect which became very popular in Tibet and has remained the most important sect upto the present day.

(50)

WHITE TARA

Tara is the female deity of the Buddhist Pantheon. White Tara was born from a tear of the Boddhisatwa of compassion, Avalokiteswora. She holds a very prominent position in Tibet and Nepal. Tara is believed to protect the human beings while they are crossing the ocean of existence.

Among the two forms of Tara, White Tara is regarded as consort of Avalokiteswara, some times of Vairochana. She is portrayed usually seated, dressed and crowned like a Boddhisatwas. And sometime she is regarded as Saptalochana or seven eyes Tara. Extra eyes on her forehead, palm, and feet and lotus flower at one or both of her shoulder. She is seated in full Vajra Posture. Her right hand will be in boon confering posture, her left hand in teaching gesture holding the stem of the lotus. She is wearing all sorts of precious ornaments and looks beautiful. The practice of White Tara is basically performed in to prolong life as well as for healing purpose.

SRISTIKANTA LOKESWARA

Sristikanta Lokeswara is also a form of Avalokiteswar. He is one faced and two-armed and stands on a lotus. He displays the Varada pose with his right hand, while his empty left hand rest near his navel. A large number of four-armed gods issue from various part of his body. Amitabha appears over his head.

SHIVA

Shiva is a Hindu God. He is the destroyer and regenerator. He is believed to have three forms. Natraj the God of Dancing skill, an anthromorphic form and the lingam form. In front of any Shiva temple, one usually sees a statue of Nandi, the divine bull that serve as Shiva's vehicle. In anthropomorphic form, Shiva is depicted with his consort Parbati and usually holds a trident and a small drum. Another popular form of Shiva is the terrifying.

SHIMHANADA LOKESHARA

Shimhanada Lokeswara is one of the forms of 108 Avalokiteswara. He is regarded by the Mahayanist as the curer of all deseases. He appears in many forms only slightly different from one another. He is of white complexion, with three eyes, and the Jatanmukuta (Crown of matted hair). He is without ornaments, is clad in tiger skin, and sits on a lion. In his right there is a white trident entwined by a white snake. From his left hand rises a lotus on which there is sword burning like fire.

SAMBARA

Sambara means "Supreme Bliss". It covers wide system of meditation instruction, yogic practices, and other spiritual exercises teaching the way towards inner freedom. Sambara will have 12 arms, four heads each with 3 three eyes. There will be various symbolic objects holding in his hands. His consort is Vajravarahi united with him in a mystic embracing position.

VARAHI

Varahi is a boarface goddess who protects temples and Buildings. Four Varahi are said to preside over the four quarters of Kathmandu Valley. Vajravarahi, red in color presides over the west and proteets livestock.; Nilavarahi, blue in color, guards the east; Swetavarahi, white in color, watches over the south; Dhumbarahi, grey in color, guards the north and protects the valley from cholera.

VASUNDHARA

Vasundhara is the Goddess of wealth or abundance as like her Brahmanic counter part Laxmi. She is portrayed on sitting on a double lotus pedestal in a posture similar to Tara. She has four hands holding a sheaf of paddy, a full Vase (purna Kalasa), a bundle of Jewels and exhibits Varada Mudra in right hand. She has three faces brown in right, redish in left and yellow in the centre. She is like Laxmi in Hindu Mythology.

VISHNU

Vishnu is a Hindu God who is also known as Narayan. Vishnu is the protector of universe and all the creatures of the Universe. He is believed to have visited the earth ten times as 'Avtars' or incarnations to save the world from destruction. He is commonly depicted as a regal figure standing firm and erect and holding four attributes; the conch, the club, lotus and wheel. His mount is mythical Bird, Garuda. His counterpart is Goddess Laxmi, the goddess of wealth.

YAMA

Yama, king and judge of the dead, is believed to sit in the centre of the regions of hell. The wicked are brought before him to be questioned and judged and are then conducted to their punishment by demons. Yama has three forms. One form has a bull's head, third eye, and crown of skulls, behind which his hair rise in flame shape. He steps to the right on the bull under which is a woman and holds a chopper in his right hand skull cup in his left. The second form is with a bull's head, third eye, crown of skulls, hair rising in flame shape and is naked, but has a belt of heads and many jewels, sometime he is represented with his sister yami at his left holding a skull cup. On his breast is an ornament representing the Buddhist wheel. In the third form he is judge of hell. He is like the above except that he steps to the left on a man.

YAMANTAKA

Yamantaka is the conqueror of Death (Yama). He is the ferocious emanation of Manjushree. Under this form he conquered the demon king of Death (Yama). The simplest form of Yamantaka has one bull head and two arms. He has a crown of skulls and the third eye. In his right hand is a chopper and left a skull cup. He has a belt of heads and steps to the right. In painting he is represented with sexteen feet, thirty four arms holding all the Tantra symbols and nine heads.

ASTAMATRIKAS

According to the Hindu Mythology Astamatrikas are the devine mother goddesses or saktis. They are variously counted as seven, eight or ten. When they are eight in numbers they are Asta matrikas. They are related with the theme of struggle between the forces of knowledge and the forces of ignorance.

BODHISATWA

Avalokiteswara is famous as a Bodhisatwa emanating from the Dhyani Buddha, Amitabha and his consort 'Pandora'. He is said to be the Bodhisatwa who rules during the period between the disappearance of the Mortal Buddha, Sakyashimha and the advent of the future Buddha Maitreya. Bodhisatwa refused Niravana until all created beings should be in possesion of the Bodhi Knowledge and to that end he is still supposed to work and foster spiritual knowledge amongst his fellow creatures.

BRAHMA

He is the creator of all worldly things. Brahma's consort is Saraswati, the goddess of creative arts. The four main castes of Hinduism are related to the parts of Brahma's body from which they originated. The Brahmins came from his head, the Khestriyas from his arms, the Vaisyas, the traders and farmers from his thighs and the Sudras class from his feet.

HANUMAN

Hanuman is a monkey faced god. He aided Rama to destroy Ravana, the ten headed demon king. He is often found in pictures with Sita and Rama or statues by himself. In Nepal, his images are usually covered with a thick vermillion mixed with mustard oil and often dressed in a red cloth with red or golden umbrella over his head. He is especially venerated by princes and warriors.

MAHASAMBER

Mahasamber is the Buddhist Gaurdian God known as 'The Great Defender'. He has seventeen heads in five rows four in each row and one at the top. The main head of the four in each row faces the front and is blue on the right and green on the left. The heads on the blue side are yellow and the pairs of heads on the green side are blue green and red. The heads are larger at the bottom and smaller at the top. All the faces are demonic i.e. square shaped with three bulging eyes, heavy eye brows, gaping mouth and fangs. The colour division of the main faces is continued all the way down the body, the right half being blue, the left half green. He has two sets of 17 and 18 arms i.e. making 70 arms. There are also four main arms. In these four arms he is holding his Sakti Vajravarahi. Each of Maha Sambara's feet has six toes and he stands with legs astide in Alidhasana.

SARASWATI

Saraswati is the goddess of Learning. All those who worship her is believed to confer Wisdom and Learning. As Goddess of music and poetry she is revered alike by Brahmans and Buddhists. She is generally represented seated holding with her two hands the Bina. She is of white colour and her mount is a peacock.

SAHASRABHUJA
AVALOKITESWARA

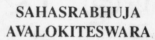

Sahasrabhuja Avalokiteswara is cosmic form of Avalokiteswara. He is represented with eleven heads and one thousand arms. The basic image is of the eleven headed and eight armed Lokeswara. The eight arms of Sahasrabhuja Avalokiteswara has more prominent position and other remaining one are distributed on either side to form a mandala. These arms are sometimes marked with eyes. The eleventh head at the top is that of his parent Tathagata, Amitabha. The tenth head is terrifying and all others are placid. The principal pair of hands is held against the chest in the gesture of adoration while the uppermost hands hold the rosary and the full blown lotus. These four hands thus represent the aspect of the Bodhisatwa known as Kharchheri. The other four hands display the jewel and the gesture of charity on the right and the pot and the bow and arrow on the left.

RAHULA

Rahula is the Dharma Protector. He is arisen out of the pure land of fire and infinite ferocity. He is smoky grey in colour. He has nine heads, four arms and one thousand flaming eyes.

KHARACHHERI

Kharchheri is also a form of Bodhisatwa Avalokiteswara. He is also known as Six Syllabled Lokeswara. The Six syllables are "OM MANI PADME HUM" which is considered so efficacious that it has been carved on rock faces and constantly chanted by devotees. He is always decked with all sorts of ornaments. He is white in colour, four armed carrying rosary in the right hand and full blown lotus in left. The other two principal hands are raised to the chest with the palms enjoined in Namaskar Mudra with a round object known as "Jewel" which is regarded as a symbol of knowledge.

NARTESWARA

Shiva, when in the form of dancing is known as Narteswara. He has fourteen arms and mostly found on his mount, Bull. Narteswara is the Nepali counterpart of famous south Indian Nataraj (King of Dancers). Narteswara is very popular with the Newars as Naasan Deva, patron of music and dance.

AKASHAGARBHA

The Bodhisatwa Akashagarbha is also known by the name of Khagarbha. The word "KHA" and "Akasha" signify the same thing "SKY". Akashagarbha is the Bodhisatwa who lives in the world of Sky.

Akashagarbha is green in complexion with the right hand shows all kinds of jewels and with the left he holds the Cintamani (wish giving) jewel.

VIGHNANTAKA

Vighnantaka is a gaurdian god of the gates in the Mandala. The name is significant as the word "Vighna" or "Obstacle" refers to the Hindu God Ganesh. He is one faced, two armed, and blue in colour. He carries in his left hand the Tarjanipasa and wields the Vajra in the right. He is terrible in appearance and his brown hair rises upwards. There is a prostrate figure of Ganesh whom he tramples under his feet. It is said that the god Ganesh, being strongly opposed to the idea, began threwing dangerous obstacles on the way of the due performance of the rite of the Odiyana Pandit in order to obtain Siddhi (perfection). Being helpless the Odiyana Pandit invoked the god Vighnantaka, the destroyer of all obstacles. Vighnantaka appreared in a fierce and terrible form, armed with destructive weapons and in no time overcome the latter. So, it may be seen how Vighnantaka is trampling heavily on Ganesh.

APARMITA
(AMITAYUS)

Aparmita is the name given to Amitabha in his charactor of bestower of longevity. Aparmita may be turned either a "Crowned Buddha or a Bodhisatwa and is therefore richly clad and wears the thirteen ornaments. His hair is painted blue and falls on either side to his elbows or may be curiously coiled. He is seated like a Buddha and his hands lie on his lap in Dhyana Mudra holding the ambrosia vase, his special emblem. The vase is richly decorated and from the cover fall four strings of beads which represent sacred pills.

For obtaining long life the lamaist ceremony is held in a curious mixture of Buddhism and demon-worship. In the preliminary worship, the pills made from buttered dough and the ambrosia brewed from spirit or beer and offered in a skull bowl to the great image of Aparmita.

The lama then places a vajra on the ambrosia vase, which the image of Amitayus holds in its lap, and applies a cord, which is attached to the vajra, to his own heart. The wine in the ambrosia vase is then consecrated and the people partake of it as well as of the sacred pills with the firm conviction that their lives will be prolonged through their faith in Aparmita.

BISWAPANI

Biswapani is very obscure. One seldom finds representation of the god either in bronze or paintings. He is seated, dressed in all the Bodhisatwa ornaments. His left hand lying on his lap, palm turned upward. The right hand in charity mudra holds his symbol the double thunderbolt. Viswapani is believed to be in contemplation before the Adi Buddha while waiting the fifth cycle when he will create the fifth world to which Maitriya will come as Manushi Buddha.

UMA MAHESWARA

Uma Maheswara is another name of Parvati and Shiva. When Shiva is represented with his consort Parvati or Uma, in composition called Uma Maheswara. In this position Shiva, Maheswara is shown sitting in a relaxed posture (Lalitasana) in his home Mount Kailash with his wife Uma as she sits on his left thigh and resting in the body of Nandi his mount at his right side. He has four arms, the top right holding a string of beads (Akshyamala) and the top left a trident (Trisula). The front right hand is turned downwards in the gesture of bestowing (Varada mudra) while the left is under the left shoulder of Uma. His hair is shaped in Jata, that is braided and piled high in the characteristic style of an ascetic. Uma is nestling on her husband's left thigh with her right hand. Her left leg raised on the seat. The lower part of her body is turned gracefully outwards with her right foot hanging down and resting on the back or her tiny mount, the lion. Uma is holding a flower in her left hand. The Uma Maheswara composition became a prototype representation of a peaceful aspects of Shiva and Parvati.

BHAISAJYA (MEDICINE) BUDDHA

Bhaisajyaguru is known as Medicine Buddha. He is also called the Healing Buddha. He is said to dispense spiritual medicine when properly worshipped. It is even believed that an efficacious cure may be accomplished by merely touching the image. In Tibet, he may be represented either as a Buddha or as a Bodhisatwa. As a Buddha, he has the urn (small round bulge or protuberance above the bridge of the nose) the fourth superior marks of a Buddha Ushnisha (A buldge or protuberance in the skull of the Buddha the first superior marks of a Buddha) short and curly hair. He wears a monastic robe, is seated with the legs crossed. His left hand lying in his lap In meditation mudra, usually holds the medicine bowl, while the right hand in charity mudra holds either a branch with fruit, or the fruit alone, of the myrobalan, as medicinal plant found in India and other tropical countries.

VIDHYADHARI

Vidhyadhari is a spirit, or demigod possessed of knowledge or magic powers, she is one of the Tantric group of four females, skilled in yoga. She has two arms and two legs. Her right leg is bent upwards at the knee so that she is not touching corpse that is lying face down beneath her. At the same time she has thrown her left leg so high that it is actually backwards. This performance shows that she is a slim young woman. She has a splendid crown, round earrings, chains round her neck and over breast and bends round her upper arms, wrists and ankles. From her shoulders hangs a long garland of human skulls. She has raised her left hand so if to drink from a bowl made out of a human skull with blood. In her right hand carries a chopper.

BAJRAGANDHARI

Bajragandhari is one of the terrible goddess endowed with six faces and twelve arms. She is blue in colour with brown hair rising upwards. She stands in the Pratyalidha attitude. Her faces look terrible with bare fangs and three eyes. She carries in her six right hands, the vajra, the bell marked with a vajra, the sword, the trident, the arrow and the disc. In her six left hands she carries Khartwanga, the goad, the bow, the parasu, the noose and the tarjani against the chest. Her first face is blue and the other five faces show five different colours.

NAIRATMA

The word 'Nairatma' means 'having no soul' and is another name for Surya. The forms of Nairatma is in many respects similar to the form of Vajravarahi, she is blue in colour while Vajravarahi is red in colour. Vajravarahi is emanation of Vairochana so there should be the image of Vairochana on the crown; while Nairatma, being an emanation of Akshyobhya, should bear the image of Akshyobhta on the crown. Like Vajravarahi she stands in the Ardhapayanka in a dancing attitude on the moon over the chest of a corpse. Her face looks terrible with bare fangs and protruding tongue. She carries the Katri in the right hand and bears the Kapala and the Khartwanga in the left.

RATNAPANI

He is the Bodhisatwa of Dhyani Byddha Ratna Sambhava. He is green in colour, holds the jewel in the right hand, and the disc of the moon on lotus in the left hand.

MANJUVAJRA

Manjuvajra is a form of Manjusri represented with his sakti. He has three heads. The centre face is red, the right face is blue and the left white. He has six arms which the principal pair is engaged in embracing his female counter part. The remaining four hands carry the sword, the arrow, the bow and the night lotus. He sits in Vajrasana or in the Bajra-Paryanka attitude in the orb of the moon supported by a lotus

YOGAMBAR

Yogambara is the principal deity of Yogamber Mandala. He sits in Ardhaparyanka on a double lotus placed on lion. He is blue in colour and is three faced. His principal face is blue, the right white and the left red. He is six armed. In his two principal hands carrying the Vajra and the Vajra marked bell. He embraces his prajna jnan dakini, who is either blue or white in colour and is decked in ornaments of snake. In the remaining two hands he holds the breast and the arrow, and in the two left he shows the lotus bowl and the bow.

CROWN BUDDHA

Crown Buddha is a Buddha in the position of meditation known as firm as a diamond. He is making the gesture of "Touching the earth" Gesture and attitude are equally characteristic of the historic Buddha Sakyamuni and of his earthly predecessors, and of the Dhyani Buddha Akshobhya, the unshakable one.

CHAMUNDA

Chamunda is the sixth deity in the series of Hindu mother goddesses which are known as Astamatrikas. Chamunda rides on a corpse. She is of red colour and four armed with the first pair of hands. She holds the katri in the right and the kapala in the left. In the second she exhibits the anjali Chamunda, known also as Kali, is the celebrated Hindu goddess of death. She may be represented alone or in the Company of a group of goddesses known collectively as the Eight Mother goddesses. She was created by the great goddess Durga who gave her title Chamunda, because she killed the demons Chanda and Munda. Her body is bare and very thin with fantastic and expressive face articulated ribs bony arms and legs.

VAJRAPANI

Vajrapani with the vajra symbol is the spiritual son of the Dhyani Buddha Akshobhya who is the progenitor of the Vajra family. His spiritual mother is Mamaki. Vajrapani is also known as god of rain. It is said that when the Nagas (serpent) appeared before Buddha to listen to his teachings, Vajrapani was charged by Tathagata to guard them from the attacks of their mortal enemies, the Garudas. To deceive and combat the Garudas, Vajrapani assumed a form with head, wings and claws like the Garuda themselves. Hence, Vajrapani as the protector of Nagas is looked upon as the Rain God. So, Northern Buddhists appeal when rain is needed or is too abundant. One can also find Vajrapani in Garuda form among the various forms of Vajrapani. Vajrapani when represented either stands or sits and carries usually a lotus on which is placed the family symbol of Vajra. Sometime, he holds the vajra against the chest in one of his hands.

CHHEPU

Chhepu is one among the three brothers Garuda, Chhepu and Hitimanga. It is told that once the mother of these brothers, requested her husband to give birth of such a son who would be the bravest, most truthful and entitled with all superior marks. Her husband told her to wait for a certain period. She being impatience to wait for a long period, looked the nest whether he was born or not. She found Chhepu in a prematured condition only with formation of head.

It is also told that Chhepu disappeared from the world as he did not want to see the kaliyuga, the great yuga, when the evil would completely trumphant over the good and the world would be destroyed by Vishnu in his incarnation as kalki, the destroyer. Knowing his bravery, truthfulness and entitled with all the superior marks Manjushree wanted to see him and requested Chhepu to show his full form. Chhepu appeared slowly amidst the cloud. Manjushree, as an veteran artist, immediately drew his form by his foot secretly without the knowledge of Chhepu. When Manjushree could finish to draw his head only Chhepu came to know Manjushree's deception and immeditely disappeared. Due to his bravery, truthfulness and all superior marks, he was given the place at the top of the main entrance of the shrines for the protection from all the dangers. Nagas are the food of Chhepu.

KSITIGARBHA

The third Bodhisatwa Ksitigarbha is rarely represented. He is yellow in colour, shows the earth touching mudra in the right hand, a lotus with the wish giving tree (Kalpa Briksha) in the left.

Simbasya

ANIMAL FACED GODDESSES

There is a set of four very interesting deities. They all have animal faces and have several forms such as (a) Hayashya with horse faced, (b) Sukarasya with sow faced; (c) Svanasya with dog faced and (d) Simbasya with lion faced. Each of them has given a different direction in the Mandala such as Hayasya in eastern gate, Sukarasya in the southern gate, Svanasya in the western gate and Simbasya in the northern gate. They are voilent in appearance, nude, dancing on a corpse and wearing garlands of severed heads. They carry the kartri in the right hand and kapala in the left hand.

Kakasya

BIRD FACED GODDESSES

There is another set of four very interesting deities. They all have bird faces and have several forms such as (a) Kakasya-crow faced; (b) Grishasya-Vulture faced; (c) Garudasya-Garuda faced and (d) Ulukasya-Owl faced. Each of them has given the intermediate corners of the Mandala. All of them are violent in appearance, nude, dancing on a corpse and wearing garlands of severed heads. They carry the kartri in the right hand and the kapala in the left hand.

DHARMADHATU

The term 'Dharmadhatu' has different meanings according to different context. The literal meaning of the term is explained as 'Source of Dharmas' or elements of dharmas. It is the non-sencious object of element perceived when we are free of thought constructs.

According to Swayambhu Purana text, the words Swayambhu, Dharmadhatu, Sunyarupa etc.

(65)

are used as synonyms. Swayambhu is called self existent wisdom or Primordial awareness. When manifested in physical form, it is known as Adi Buddha. In Nispannayogavali Dharmadhatu Mandala is described in great detail. In this mandala chief deity is Manjughosha, the representative of Primordial Awareness with four faces and eight arms. A large number of deities are included in this Mandala. The devotee is allowed to visualize this Mandala in developing stage of meditation. By this practice the devotee swiftly accumulates the merits and wisdom necessary for the attainment of Buddhahood.

MAHAKALA

Several series of Hindu deties are found in the Buddhist Pantheon. Mahakala is one of the Hindu deties of Brahma group. He is one of the eight terrible deities of the Buddhist pantheon with ornaments of snakes, canine teeth, protuding belly and dressed with tiger skin. He is dark blue in colour. He carries trisula and kapala in his two hands. He may have one face with two, four or six arms or eight faces with sixteen arms. As he is the defender of law, he is given a good position at the entrance doors of Buddhist Shrines.

MAHAPARATISARA

Mahapratisara is one of the principal deities of Pancha Raksha. She occupies the center of the Mandala. She protects from all sorts of specific evils and physical dangers. She is to be conceived as having the image of Ratna Sambhava in her crown.

She has four faces. The front face is yellow, the right is white, the rear is blue and the left is red in colour. This deity has twelve arms. In her six right arms she holds the jewel, the discus, the vajra, the arrow, the noose, the trident, the bow, the axe and the conch.

NAGARJUN

Nagarjun is usually called the 'Founder' of the Mahayan system. Some claimed that he was only its principal expounder. Some look upon Asvaghosha, the probable master of Nagarjuna as the founder of Mahayan doctrine. Others still believe that Nagarjun founded the Madhyamika School and was the first to teach the Amitabha doctrine.

Nagarjun was born in Southern India around the end of the second century A. D. His parents were of the Brahman caste. At his birth, it was predicated that he would only live seven days. Considering the acts of merit performed by his parents, the god delayed his death until seven weeks and then seven months and finally to seven years. Before the seven years were up, he was sent to Nalanda where he learnt to adore Amitayus, god of long life, and succeeded to propitiate the god and lived three hundred years on earth.

Nagarjuna was the greatest Buddhist philosopher and mastered all the sciences, and especially magic Art. He is said to have acquired Siddhi by which magic power he obtained the Rainbow body' and was thus able to become invisible at will and transport himself from one place to another by supernatural power. Different Buddhists claim Nagarjuna about his rank as the disciple of the Buddha.

According to Buddhist texts, Sakyamuni predicated the rebirth of his disciple Ananda under the name of Nagarjuna founder of the Mahayana System.

Some believed that Nagarjuna received the doctrine directly from Vajrasatwa. Some believed that he received the treatise from the serpent gods, the Nagas to whom Gautam Buddha had given the treatise until such time as the world should become sufficiently enlightened to understand its transendent wisdom.

Nagarjun was deified and enroled among the Northern Buddhist divinities. He has a halo on which are seven snakes. If painted, the middle one is yellow and the others grey. He is represented like a Buddha. he wears the monastic garments. He has no symbols. His hands are in dharmachakra mudra. If painted, he is white.

OM !

Om, the mystic syllable of A-u-m is venerated by the Brahmans as well as by the Buddhist. The devotees regard it to be too sacred to be uttered aloud only formed by the lips. It is written that when all was void the triliteral syllable Aum became manifest.

Adi Buddha at his will proceeded from Om. In that Aum, Adi Buddha who is present in all things formless and passionless, possesses the Tri-Ratna. It is also written that Adi Buddha became manifest in the greatest Sunyata (void) as the letter A. It is also written that when all was Sunyata, Prajna Devi (Adi Dharma) was revealed out of Akasa with the letter 'U'. The Vija mantra of Sangha is 'M'. Thus the letters A-u-m are the vija mantra of Buddha. Dharma and Sangha V. Tri-Ratna.

The mantra generally begins with Om and ends with hum. the most widely known mantra is the six syllable one of Avalokiteswara 'Om Mani Padme Hum'.

PANCHA RAKSHYA

Pancha Rakshya Deities are five protectresses deities popular and well known amongst the Mahayana Buddhist particularly of Nepal. A manuscript copy of the Pancha Rakshya describing five Rakshya deities, their worship on different occasion and their powers is found in every Buddhist house of Nepal. It is stated that when these five Rakshya deities are worshipped grant a long life. They protect kingdom, villages and meadows. They protect men from evil spirits, diseases and famines. This manuscript is recited in all varieties of domestic difficulties such as illness, ill fortunes, loss of wealth etc.

All the deities are worshipped either singly or collectively in a Mandala. In the Pancha Rakshya Mandala Mahapratisara is enthroned in the centre while four others occupy the four direction such as Mahasahasrapramardini in the east Mahamantranusarini in the south, Mahasitavati in the west and Mahamayuri in the north. It is also said that any one of the deities may become a leader in the Mandala occupying the central position. In this case all other deities become her subordinates.

KURUKULLA

There are many forms of the deity Kurkulla. But the most important form is called Tarodbhava. She is the goddess of wealth. She is also worshipped by unhappy lovers. She is believed to be successful in bewitching men, women, ministers, and the kings. 'Om kurukulle hum hrin svaha' is the mantra when muttered ten thousand times is said to fulfil every one's desires. Thirty thousand times of this mantra must be muttered to subdue a minister. The subjugation of a king requires more than a lakh. She is red in colour with red garments, red ornaments and seated on a red lotus. She is usually represented in dancing attitude. If she stands, she stands on her left foot and her right leg is raised. She either wears a crown of skulls or a band surmounted by ornnaments. She has four arms. Two left hands show charging a flowery arrow on a flower bow ready to strike at and other two hands hold a noose and a goad.

VAJRANANGA

This form of Manjushree bearing the image of Akshyobhya on the crown is known as Vajrananga. He is worshipped in the Tantric rite of bewitching men and women. His complexion is yellow. He is in the prime of youth and bears the image of Akshyobhya on his crown. The two principal hands hold the fully expanded bow. The four remaining hands carry the sword and the looking glass in the right hands, while the two left hands carry the lotus and the Asoka bough (a particular kind of tree) with the red flowers.

HAYAGRIVA

Hayagriva is also one of the main archetype dieties of Nyingma Order. He is one of the emanation of Bidhisattwa Avalokiteswar in terrific form. He has many forms often with three faces, six arms, and four legs, and sometimes with huge wings. He can be recognised by a small horse head surmounted on the top of his main terrific head and gives him his name Hayagriva. "Horse necked one". The horse head neighs very loudly and the sound is said to pierce all the false appearance inherent existence or substantial reality. His hair is dishevelled and protuding from the horse head. He wears a crown of skulls and under a belt of heads hangs a tiger skin. His symbols are the thunderbolt, trident lasso etc.

ASTAMANGALA
(The Eight Auspicious Signs)

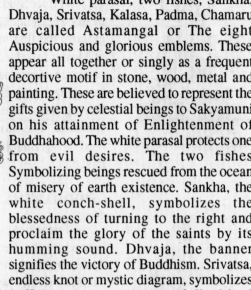

White parasal, two fishes, Sankha, Dhvaja, Srivatsa, Kalasa, Padma, Chamaru are called Astamangal or The eight Auspicious and glorious emblems. These appear all together or singly as a frequent decortive motif in stone, wood, metal and painting. These are believed to represent the gifts given by celestial beings to Sakyamuni on his attainment of Enlightenment of Buddhahood. The white parasal protects one from evil desires. The two fishes Symbolizing beings rescued from the ocean of misery of earth existence. Sankha, the white conch-shell, symbolizes the blessedness of turning to the right and proclaim the glory of the saints by its humming sound. Dhvaja, the banner signifies the victory of Buddhism. Srivatsa, endless knot or mystic diagram, symbolizes of the endless cycle of rebirth. Kalasa, the vase; treasury of all spiritual wealth and it also helds amrita the water elixir immortality Padma symbolizes of Purity. Chamaru, fly-whisk; symbolizes Tantric manifestations, it is made of yak tail attached with silver staff, it is used during ritual recitation and fanning the deities on an auspicious religious ceremony. These eight auspicious symbols usually displayed during the performance of vrata ceremonies, consecration of house and an elaborate Fire sacrifice ceremony marked on paper, cloth or metal.

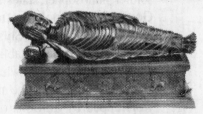

NIRVAN BUDDHA

Buddha entering into Nirvan in Kusinagar in 543 B. C. in reclining posture after 45 years of untiring efforts in preaching the path to emancipation from the bondage of suffering i. e. Birth, Old Age, Desease and Death. Three months before the full moon of the month of Magh, he had announced to the Bhikhhus in Vaisali that he was relinquishing his will to live as his body was already wornout and he would enter into Nirvana (Passing away) in Kushinagar on Bhaisakh Full Moon Day.

DEEP MEDITATING BUDDHA

Prince Shiddhartha in his emaciated posture in his engagement in deep meditation for three months, the first month spent in taking one grain of Mustard seed a day, the second month in taking one grain of sesame seed a day, and the third month in taking one grain of dry pulse (kolan) a day. During these three months, he was reduced to skeleton, The stone figure representing Deep Meditating Buddha was in Taxila, found now in Pakistan.

SIDDHARTHA WITH WOUNDED DUCK

Price Shiddhartha treating the wounded duck injured by the arrows of Prince Deva-dutta, the cousin brother of Prince Shiddhartha always claiming rivalry with the Buddha. This figure is the symbolical expression of Prince Shiddhartha's compassion towards the ailing creatures.

KRISHNA

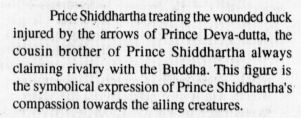

Krishna is an eight incarnation of Vishnu. Krishna was the Hero of Mahabharat. He was a soldier, philosopher, statesman and admired by the Gopinis, who looked after the cows. He had destroyed king Kansa, Shishupala and Kalya, the serpent king. He had established a new philosophy of action in Hinduism, which is known as Geeta. He is considered to be the most important god and worshipped by millions of people in India and Nepal. He became most popular and beloved hero of Hindu mythology, the symbol of devotion, love, joy and music. He is usually portrayed playing flute with his consort Radha dancing, or surrounded with milkmaids (gopinis). The devotion between Krishna and his consort Radha symbolized the ideal relation of love between the soul and god.

OM MANI PADME HUM

Om Mani Padme Hum (Hail the jewel in the lotus) is a six syllable invocation (Mantra) of Avlokiteswara one who is invoked as the savior and the Protector from danger. One who recites this Mantra, he will be saved from all dangers and will be protected. So this Mantra is widely found in every field of Mahayana Buddhism. One can find this Mantra inscribed on rocks, prayer wheels, Chaitya walls, loose stones heaped as Mani (jewels) on roads, paths, mountain passes, the approaches and exits of villages. One can find this Mantra inscribed outwardly in the prayer wheels and millions of this Mantra insides the prayer wheels. One who turns one round of this prayer wheel, it means he recites millions of this Mantra. As this Mantra saves from all dangers people used it as pendant, rings etc. for the protection.

VAJRAKILA

Vajrakilla known as Vajrakumar is the deity of the magic phurba dagger a symbol of the sharp point of wisdom fixed immobile on goodness by the power of one pointed concentration. Vajrakilla is one of the favourite tantric archetype deity used in Nyigma Order. The strange and awesome appearance helps the practitioners undertake and achieve the task of clearing away the obstructions to enlightenment.

Vajrakilla has three heads, six arms, and four legs. His three right hands except for the right front one held vajras with five and nine prongs. The right front one makes a gesture as granting boons with open palm. His three left hands hold a flaming three refuge jewel, a trident and the phurba dagger. His back is covered by the freshly flayed skin of the elephant of ignocance, where legs are

(73)

tied in front. A human skin is tied daigonally across his chest with the hands lying flat on his stomach. A rope ripples over his body with severed heads hanging by their hair. A knee length loin cloth winds around his belly belted with a tiger skin complete with tail, claws, and head. This deity wears live snakes as earrings, bracelets anklets, a cord over his chest and a hair ornament. His faces are round and small compared to the tall body. Despite the large fungs and bulging eyes, he has a likable pleasant demeanor.

SITATAPATTRA

Sitatapattra is the goddess of the victorious white parasol. She is a powerful independent deity. She is also known as Ushnishasitatapattra as she was emanated by Sakyamuni Buddha from his crown protusion (Ushnisha). Whoever does practice her Sadhana will be reborn in Amitabh's Pureland. Her sutra and mantra emanated from Buddha's Ushanisha.

She is popular with the Geluk order in particular. She has one thousand heads. Facing forward are two hundred white faces, to the right are two hundred yellow faces, behind are two hundred red faces, left are two hundred green faces, above are two hundred blue faces. Each face has three eyes and bears a vajra on top. Her body is white in colour, and covered with a hundred thousand million eyes. She has five hundred right hands, and five hundred left hands. Each holds a very sharp flaming sword. Her five hundred right legs are outstreched stepping on all forms of danger, and five hundred left legs are flexed with the feet drawn inwards stepping on.

EKAJATA

Ekajata is one of the most powerful goddesses in the Vajrayanic Pantheon. If a man listen to her mantra, he is at once freed from all obstacles, and is attended always with good fortune, his enemies are destroyed, and he becomes religiously inclined.

Ekajata is a feroceous form of Tara. In simplest form, she is represented seated, holding in her two hands the chopper and skull cup, and in her crown is an image of Akshyobhya. In other form she is represented with four to twenty four arms. She is generally standing on her left foot and her right ankle stepping on corpses. She has the third eye, she is laughing horribly with prominent teeth, and protruding tongue. Her eyes are red and round. Her hips are covered by a tiger skin, and she wears a long garland of heads. If painted her colour is blue. She is dwarf and corpulent. If she has four arms, her symbols are sword, knife, blue lotus and a skull cup.

SYAMBOLS AND CHARACTERSTICS OF DHYANI BUDDHA

FAMILY HEAD	Vairochana	Akshobhya	Ratna sambhava	Amitabha	Amoghashiddhi
DIRECTION	Centre	East	South	West	North
COLOUR	White	Blue	Yellow	Red	Green
MUDRA	Dharmachakra	Bhumisparsa	Varada	Dhyana	Abhaya
SYMBOL	Wheel	Thunderbolt	Jewel	Lotus	Double Thunder bolt
EMBODIMENT OF	Sovereignty	Steadfastness	Compassion	Light	Dauntlessness
TYPE OF EVIL	Stupidity	Wrath	Desire	Malignity	Envy
VEHICLES	Dragon	Elephant	Lion	Peacock	Harpys (Garuda)
SPIRITUAL SON	Manjushree	Bajrapani	Ratnapani	Avalokiteswara	Bajrapani
CONSORT	White Tara	Locana	Mamaki	Pandara	Green Tara
COSMIC ELEMENT	Form (Rupa)	Conciousness (Vijnana)	Sensation (Vendana)	Name (Sanjna)	Conformation (Samskara)

REFERENCE

1. The Gods of Northern Buddhism by Alice Getty.

2. The Indian Buddhist Iconography by Benoytosh Bhattacharya.

3. Nepal Art Treasures from the Himalayas by Ernst and Rose Leonore waldschmilt.

4. The Gods of Nepal by Mary Rubel.

5. The Gods and Goddesses of Nepal by Ceoffrey Detmold and Mary Rubel.

6. "Tantra" The Indian cult of Ecstasy by Philips Rawson.

7. Nepal Sanskritiya Mulukha by Hem Raj Shakya.

8. The Art of Nepal by Lydia Aran.

9. Art of Tibet by Pratapaditya Pal.

10. The Sacred Art of Tibet by Marylin M. Rhie and Robert A.F. Thurman

11. The Iconography of Nepalese Buddhism by Min Bahadur Shakya

12. Buddhist Himalaya Journals.